Collins

Caribbean
Social Studies 3
Workbook

Jain Cook

Collins

William Collins' dream of knowledge for all began with the publication of his first book in 1819.

A self-educated mill worker, he not only enriched millions of lives, but also founded a flourishing publishing house. Today, staying true to this spirit, Collins books are packed with inspiration, innovation and practical expertise. They place you at the centre of a world of possibility and give you exactly what you need to explore it.

Collins. Freedom to teach.

Published by Collins
An imprint of HarperCollins*Publishers*
The News Building
1 London Bridge Street
London
SE1 9GF

Browse the complete Collins Caribbean catalogue at
www.collins.co.uk/caribbeanschools

10 9 8 7 6 5 4 3 2 1

ISBN 978-0-00-825651-7

British Library Cataloguing in Publication Data
A catalogue record for this publication is available from the British Library.

Author: Jain Cook
Publisher: Dr Elaine Higgleton
Commissioning editor: Bruce Nicholson
In-house senior editor: Julianna Dunn
Project manager: Alissa McWhinnie, QBS Learning
Copyeditor: Tanya Solomons
Proofreader: Helen Bleck
Cover designer: Gordon MacGilp
Series designer: Kevin Robbins
Cover photo: Darryl Brooks/Shutterstock
Typesetter: QBS Learning
Production controller: Tina Paul
Printed and bound by: Grafica Veneta SpA in Italy

The publishers gratefully acknowledge the permission granted to reproduce the copyright material in this book. Every effort has been made to trace copyright holders and to obtain their permission for the use of copyright material. The publishers will gladly receive any information enabling them to rectify any error or omission at the first opportunity.

MIX
Paper from
responsible sources
FSC™ C007454

FSC
www.fsc.org

This book is produced from independently certified FSC™ paper to ensure responsible forest management.

For more information visit: www.harpercollins.co.uk/green

Contents

1   Our heritage

1 **Complete the sentences based on your reading of 1.1 in the Student's Book.**

a) National icons are **i)** _____ who have contributed
   ii) _____ to the development of a country. They are
   usually individuals whose life's work has been **iii)** _____
   to a particular **iv)** _____ such as sports, politics,
   science, art or culture. Through their work they have demonstrated
   v) _____ and a love for their country.

b) Sir Errol Barrow became the Premier of Barbados in 1961. Following
   i) _____ in 1966 he became Prime Minister. He expanded
   free **ii)** _____ and set up National Health Insurance. He was
   a major supporter of regional **iii)** _____ and trade, and
   co-founded CARIFTA.

c) Sir John Compton was the first **i)** _____ of St Lucia. He
   ii) _____ the United Workers Party (UWP) in 1964 and
   led the country to **iii)** _____. He returned to politics after
   retirement to lead the UWP to **iv)** _____ in 2006.

d) Sir Lester Bird was **i)** _____ of Antigua from 1994 to 2004.
   He is credited with the **ii)** _____ of Antigua's service
   industry through tourism and financial services and helped to raise the
   standard of **iii)** _____ of Antiguans. He served as
   iv) _____ to both the Organisation of Eastern Caribbean
   States (OECS) and CARICOM.

e) Who is said to have brought the Dominican musical style Kadans to
   international popularity?

   _____

f) Who is also known as 'King Onyan'?

   _____

g) Who helped to establish the Barbados Dance Project?

   _____

h) What are Kim Collins, Kirani James and Laverne Spencer famous for?

   _____

2 **Answer the questions based on your reading of 1.2 in the Student's Book.**

a) In what sport did Leah Martindale represent Barbados at two Olympic Games (1996, 2000)?

_____

b) Who was the first female West Indian cricketer to score 100 in a test match?

_____

c) Which tennis player has received the award of St Lucian Sportsman of the year and the International Tennis Federation Davis Cup Commitment Award?

_____

d) Which sport did Adonal Foyle participate in?

_____

e) What is Sir Vivian Richards recognised as?

_____

f) Which trade union did Hubert Nathaniel Critchlow help to establish?

_____

g) Name the first General Secretary of the St Kitts and Nevis Trades and Labour Union.

_____

h) What type of work does Andrew Simmons do?

_____

i) What scientific field does Leonard O'Garro specialise in?

_____

j) Who has done groundbreaking work in the field of cancer research?

_____

3 Match each person to their two achievements.

a) Hubert Nathaniel Critchlow _____

b) Joseph Nathaniel France _____

c) Andrew Simmons _____

d) Kathleen Coard _____

e) Leonard O'Garro _____

i) They founded the JEMS Progressive Community Organisation.

ii) Their work led to advances in cancer research and cardiovascular disease.

iii) They are a well-known plant pathologist.

iv) They were known as the father of the trade union movement in Guyana.

v) They are noted for their negotiation for recognition of workers' rights in the sugar industry.

vi) She was the first female professor of pathology in the Caribbean.

vii) They were the first General Secretary of the St Kitts and Nevis Trades and Labour Union.

viii) They are an environmentalist.

ix) They established the British Guiana Labour Union.

x) Their research has led to the implementation of crop disease control programmes across the Caribbean.

4 Read 1.3 in the Student's Book. Use the internet and do some research about the work of Oscar Allen. Write a short article of 200 words about his achievements with ARWE and the group People's Movement for Change.

5 Read 1.3 in the Student's Book and put the following events into the correct date order. Add the date of the event on the write-on line to help you.

a) **Garth St Omer** _____

i) *Shades of Grey* _____

ii) *Nor Any Country* _____

iii) *J–, Black Bam and the Masqueraders* _____

iv) *A Room on the Hill* _____

v) *Syrop* _____

b) Caryl Phillips _____

   i) *A State of Independence* _____

   ii) *Crossing the River* _____

   iii) *The European Tribe* _____

   iv) *The Atlantic Sound* _____

   v) *The Final Passage* _____

   vi) *A Distant Shore* _____

6 Read 1.4 in the Student's Book. Circle the letter of the word or phrase that best completes each sentence.

a) Calypso music has roots in _____ tribal songs of the eighteenth century and became popular in the early twentieth century.

   i) Indian
   ii) West African
   iii) Indo-Caribbean
   iv) Trinidadian

b) _____ music, is a fusion of the typical calypso sound with funk, soul, reggae and other musical styles.

   i) calypso
   ii) soca
   iii) chutney
   iv) reggae

c) _____ is known as the place where steel band originated.

   i) Jamaica
   ii) Guyana
   iii) Barbados
   iv) Trinidad and Tobago

d) Chutney music developed in the southern Caribbean territories, such as Trinidad and Guyana, among those of _____ descent.

    i) Indian

    ii) Jamaican

    iii) Indo-Caribbean

    iv) West Indian

e) Bouyon is a musical form developed by _____ singers which found mass appeal across the French Antilles.

    i) Dominican

    ii) Trinidadian

    iii) Tobagonian

    iv) Jamaican

7 **Read 1.5 and 1.6 in the Student's Book. Complete each sentence with one word or expression in each blank.**

poaching	infusion	physical resources	unsustainable
ecotourism	natural resources		preservation

a) In the Eastern Caribbean, our _____, such as oceans, lakes, waterfalls, flora and fauna, have helped to develop the tourism industry and to attract tourists.

b) _____ activities will make our heritage unavailable to future generations.

c) The _____ of sea turtles, hawksbills and green turtles in the East Caribbean has now become a huge problem.

d) _____ are valuable and essential to the economic development of a country.

e) _____ is a type of tourism that focuses on protecting the environment and local culture.

f) Conservation and _____ of our resources now will enable our region to leave a legacy for future generations.

g) The _____ of external cultures is a threat to our natural heritage.

8 Complete the crossword. All the words are key vocabulary words from 1.1–1.5 in the Student's Book.

Across

3. All the plants that grow in a particular region
4. A female singer of traditional creole music
5. A non-standard version of French spoken in Caribbean countries with a French colonial history
6. The influence of an external culture introduced at the expense of a nation's own cultural diversity
10. At risk of being harmed or destroyed
11. Any improvements made to a country's trade or industry
12. A type of song with lyrics usually about politics
13. An individual or group recognised for their significant contribution to the national heritage of their country (8, 4)

Down

1. A storyteller
2. Man-made resources, such as buildings (8, 9)
5. Illegally catching or killing an animal, bird or fish on someone else's property
7. All the animals that live in a particular area
8. No longer existing
9. An organisation formed by employees to protect their rights

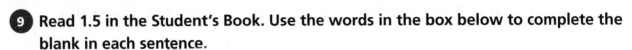
9 Read 1.5 in the Student's Book. Use the words in the box below to complete the blank in each sentence.

research	ecosystems	natural resources
protecting	disposal	poaching	educating
slash-and-burn	pollution	warming	organisations

Environmental Protection Agency Guyana

The responsibilities of the EPA-Guyana include:

a) _____ the public about the sustainable use of Guyana's natural resources

b) _____ plant and animal life

c) hazardous waste _____ and transport

d) protection of marine _____ and wildlife

Cayman Islands Department of Environment

The role of the Cayman Islands Department of Environment includes:

e) managing and protecting the environment and _____

f) working with _____ to fund environmental education programs

g) helping _____ scientists with environmental studies

Threats to our natural habitats

Today, threats to our natural habitats from human activities include:

h) squatting, _____ and illegal hunting

i) land clearing (fires), cattle grazing, logging, _____ agriculture, overfishing

j) drilling for oil and gas, quarrying, _____, such as oil spills and chemical leaks

k) global _____ and climate change

10 Read 1.7 and 1.8 in the Student's Book. Match the words in the circle to the correct heading.

Cultural transmission
_____
_____
_____

Standard of living
_____
_____
_____

natural resources   CARICOM

rely on each other   common goal   music and dance

tolerance   safeguard areas   strengthening   quality of life

preserve local resources   wealth of a country   job security

fresh air   cuisine   folklore

Survival
_____
_____
_____

Global cooperation
_____
_____
_____

Interdependence
_____
_____
_____

11 Read the key vocabulary in 1.6–1.8 in the Student's Book. Then find the words in the word search puzzle. The words can be horizontal, diagonal, vertical, backwards or forwards. There are 12 words to find.

E	P	F	S	U	P	F	S	P	V	E	W	A	I	C	E	T	M	S	C
C	C	S	A	P	D	Q	C	X	H	C	C	T	Q	F	V	M	T	U	T
O	K	N	K	I	U	U	D	O	V	S	H	N	I	J	J	L	L	B	N
O	G	G	E	R	G	J	B	R	N	A	Y	L	A	Y	M	T	I	W	E
P	Q	H	T	D	L	W	B	J	Z	S	F	E	L	R	U	J	Y	X	D
E	W	K	B	G	N	B	N	Z	U	O	E	M	F	R	E	B	G	L	N
R	U	F	H	B	Y	E	H	Y	Y	S	K	R	A	P	V	L	T	K	E
A	R	A	H	N	E	Z	P	T	K	S	I	L	V	P	M	V	O	S	P
T	H	Y	W	V	C	Q	I	E	V	K	T	B	P	A	U	B	U	T	E
I	G	N	I	V	I	L	F	O	D	R	A	D	N	A	T	S	L	V	D
O	I	I	I	D	A	Q	Y	H	A	R	E	Z	W	X	T	I	O	L	R
N	S	W	L	U	S	F	N	N	B	F	E	A	Q	A	P	I	O	P	E
E	D	K	Q	P	R	E	S	E	R	V	A	T	I	O	N	D	S	N	T
V	N	J	C	R	G	M	M	F	J	K	U	N	N	I	B	P	P	R	N
I	T	K	U	U	I	T	N	J	O	I	A	R	O	I	K	U	L	U	I
V	C	U	Q	S	E	K	R	N	A	B	I	L	S	Z	G	T	A	W	P
R	Z	R	S	F	T	Y	U	A	L	M	S	I	R	U	O	T	O	C	E
U	Z	I	P	D	L	W	A	E	X	Z	U	U	E	Z	Y	I	B	D	D
S	O	T	R	N	K	A	A	O	K	X	B	P	G	U	H	J	R	H	L
N	B	J	I	L	H	L	H	M	O	H	R	S	A	U	U	R	E	M	V

12 Write the words from Exercise 11 in alphabetical order.

a) _____   b) _____

c) _____   d) _____

e) _____   f) _____

g) _____   h) _____

i) _____   j) _____

k) _____   l) _____

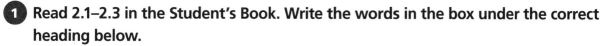

2 Economic growth and development

1 Read 2.1–2.3 in the Student's Book. Write the words in the box under the correct heading below.

satellites	communicable diseases	receiver
ebooks	social media managers	exports
the masses	software developers	markets
video call	computer networks	online
trade	electronic commerce	at our fingertips
sender	cultural creativity	internet cafés
devices	web designers	regional views
up-to-date software	imported goods	locally produced
buying products	connected	social media

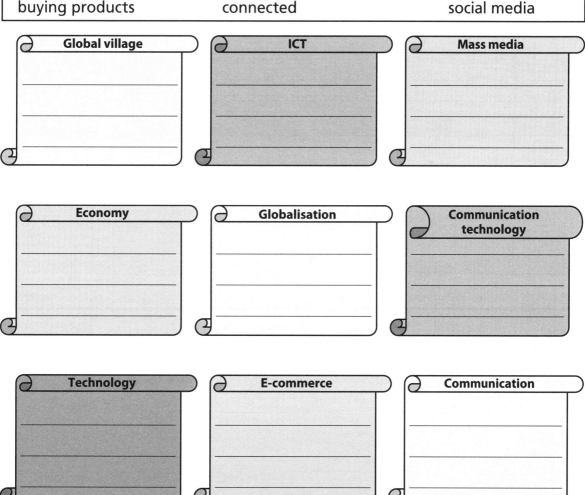

2 Complete the crossword. All the words are key vocabulary words from 2.1 and 2.2 in the Student's Book.

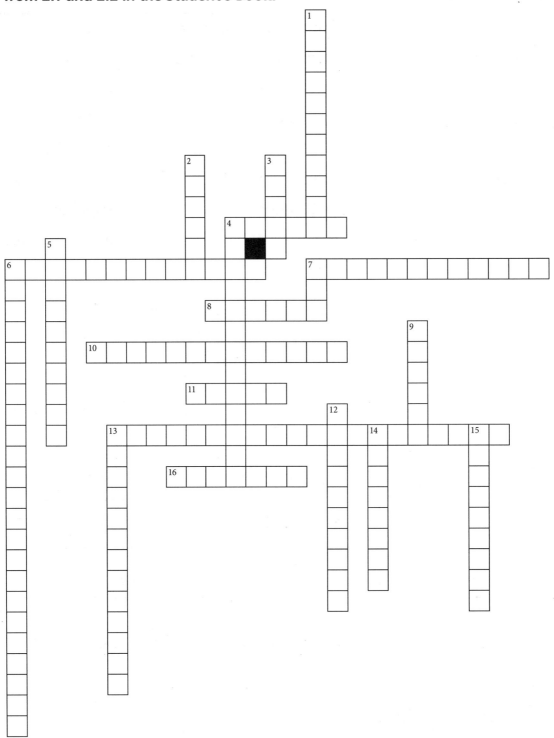

Across

4. Worldwide or relating to the whole world
6. The transfer of information between a sender and a receiver
7. Public place to access the internet (8, 4)
8. Trade in goods of a particular kind
10. Used to describe the way people all over the world have become connected through technology (6, 7)
11. Relating to the activities of buying and selling goods or services
13. Illnesses passed from one person to another, e.g. influenza (12, 7)
16. A system of how industry, trade and finance is organised in a country, region or worldwide

Down

1. New technology platforms, such as Facebook or Twitter, that allow people to interact on the Web (6, 5)
2. A mobile computing device, larger than a mobile phone
3. Written work that is available to be read digitally on an e-reader, tablet or mobile phone
4. Relating to things that take place all over the world
5. A mobile phone that also works as a small computer
6. The transfer of information between a sender and a receiver using technology (13, 10)
7. Information and communication technology
9. Connected to or available through a computer, especially the internet
12. Devices and systems which have been created for practical purposes
13. Changes that are thought to be affecting the world's weather so that it is becoming warmer (7, 6)
14. Network of millions of computers linked together that allows people all over the world to exchange information
15. Buying and selling services and products via the internet (1–8)

3 Read 2.3–2.5 in the Student's Book. Circle the word or phrase in each group below that does not belong with the rest. Say why the item you circled does not belong. Then write a sentence for each of the words/phrases that you circled.

a) i)   Increased competitiveness   _____

   ii)   Upsetting comments   _____

   iii)   Fake profile   _____

   iv)   Abusive emails   _____

b) i)   Do not reply   _____

   ii)   Keep copies   _____

   iii)   Tell someone   _____

   iv)   Economic development   _____

c) i)   Keep people connected   _____

   ii)   Can distract people   _____

   iii)   Communities come together   _____

   iv)   Businesses build relationships   _____

d) i)   Wide range of information   _____

   ii)   Online shopping   _____

   iii)   Local culture lost   _____

   iv)   Raises awareness   _____

e) i)   Buy and sell goods   _____

   ii)   Increased competition   _____

   iii)   Job creation   _____

   iv)   Decreased production   _____

4 Unscramble the words and match them with the correct definition below. All the words are key vocabulary words from 2.3 and 2.4 in the Student's Book.

a) n a t i o n f o m i r d e l o v a r o

b) c l i n g y u b b l e r y

c) s m u n o o n a y

d) s y e n r a t e d

e) m i t i n a i t e d

f) s a m s d i a m e

g) b y c e r a s u b e

h) c l a s i o w r e k i g n t o n t i e s

i) s t a i n n t g n a m i g e s s

i) Involving a lot of sitting and not much exercise

ii) When someone sends or posts texts or images that are deliberately meant to hurt or embarrass someone

iii) A place to create and share information and ideas in online communities

iv) Sending messages or images to someone using the internet or a mobile phone in order to frighten or upset them

v) Deliberately make someone feel frightened

vi) When there is more information than someone can deal with, leading to stress and anxiety

vii) Newspapers, television, radio, etc. that communicate news and information to large numbers of people

viii) Something that is done, written, etc. by someone whose name is not known

ix) Communicating with someone directly over the internet and replying to their messages as soon as they arrive

5 **Read 2.5 and 2.6 in the Student's Book. Then complete the sentences about how transport systems help economic development and the global distribution of goods.**

Roads

a) The movement of goods from the place where they are **i)** _____ to places where they can be sold is **ii)** _____. They allow **iii)** _____ to get to and from work, and **iv)** _____ to move goods.

Water

b) It allows the transport of **i)** _____ and _____ items. **ii)** _____ are often naturally occurring and generally do not need many repairs. In the Caribbean, the presence of **iii)** _____ encourages tourism.

Rail

c) Rail travel can be relatively quick, as there is less congestion on the rail **i)** _____. The railways can carry **ii)** _____ and _____.

Air

d) Cargo can easily be **i)** _____ between countries or within large countries. Air travel encourages **ii)** _____.

Consumer and consumerism

e) A consumer is a person who uses **i)** _____ and _____, which may satisfy the consumer's **ii)** _____ or _____.

Distribution and marketing

f) **i)** _____ is the process through which a product or service is made available to **ii)** _____. Typically, these people form a **iii)** _____, which involves the producer, a **iv)** _____, marketing team, the **v)** _____ and then the consumer.

6 Match the words below to their definitions. All the words are key vocabulary words from 2.5 in the Student's Book.

a) competitiveness   i)   moving people or things from one place to another

b) transportation   ii)   the ability to travel from one place to another

c) mobility   iii)   offering goods or services at cheaper prices than other companies

d) port   iv)   something that works well and produces good results

e) efficient   v)   an area of water where ships stop

7 Read 2.6 in the Student's Book. Answer these questions about the distribution chain.

a) Who can be a single person or a factory?

_____

b) What does the person in question a) make?

_____

c) What example is given of something producers provide that we need?

_____

d) Producers can also provide services that we want. What examples are given?

_____

e) Who is the intermediary in the distribution chain?

_____

f) What does the person in question e) do?

_____

g) Where does this person store their goods?

_____

h) Who buys goods from a wholesaler?

_____

i) Who cannot buy directly from a wholesaler?

_____

j) When they sell goods to the public, what are retailers also called?

_____

k) What does marketing create for a product?

_____

8 Read 2.7 in the Student's Book. Answer the questions about Guyana's imports and complete the diagram.

a) What, like many countries around the world, does Guyana have to do?

_____

b) Why do countries have to do this?

_____

c) What is the main product brought into Guyana in percentage terms?

_____

d) Name the second and third highest imports into the country.

_____

e) Complete the missing information:

i) _____ 4.1%

ii) Chemical products _____ %

iii) _____ 1.9%

iv) _____ 1.4%

v) Machines _____ %

vi) _____ 23.1%

vii) Transportation _____ %

viii) Animal products _____ %

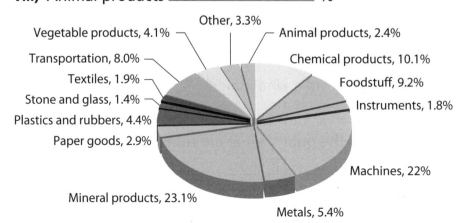

Imports into Guyana in 2016.

22

9 Read 2.7 and 2.8 in the Student's Book. Choose words from the box to complete the paragraph below.

trading agreements	goods	foreign exchange
balance of trade	products	natural resources
trade sanctions	invest	petroleum	investments

The difference in value between the exports and imports in one year is called the **i)** _____. Trinidad and Tobago has a high value of exports. However, if the price of **ii)** _____ and natural gas drops, this can affect these trade figures.

A favourable balance of trade is good for an economy because the country earns **iii)** _____, which it can use to pay for imports. In addition, the economy remains stable, which attracts **iv)** _____ and encourages entrepreneurs to **v)** _____ in new businesses. This in turn creates more job opportunities.

Exports are **vi)** _____ that are sent to other countries to be sold. They are usually subject to **vii)** _____ between different countries and to national and international laws. Countries may sometimes not be allowed to sell goods to countries on which **viii)** _____ have been imposed.

Countries export goods and **ix)** _____ that they have too much of. If a country produces more oil than it can use, then some of the oil is exported to other countries. **x)** _____ like gas and coal can also be exported to other countries that lack these resources.

Trinidad and Tobago exports more than it imports, mainly as a result of petroleum and natural gas products.

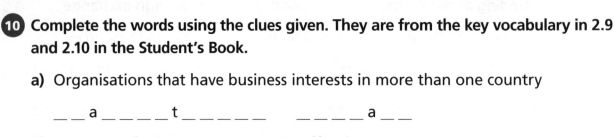
10 Complete the words using the clues given. They are from the key vocabulary in 2.9 and 2.10 in the Student's Book.

a) Organisations that have business interests in more than one country

_ _ a _ _ _ _ t _ _ _ _ _ _   _ _ _ _ a _ _

b) A system of administration run by officials

_ u _ _ a _ _ _ _ c _

c) When a company starts to sell its products

_ _ r _ _ _   _ o _ _ _

d) The set of systems within a place or organisation that affects how well it operates

_ _ _ r _ _ _ r _ _ _ _ _ _

e) Using the internet to buy goods or services

_ _ _ i _ _   _ _ _ _ _ i _ _

f) An announcement telling people about a product or service

_ _ _ e _ _ i _ _ n _

g) Place where things can be kept

_ _ o _ a _ _

11 Write 200–250 words about the shop you go to the most for clothes. Think about the following:

- Why do you shop there so often?

- Do they offer reasonable prices?

- How did you hear about the shop? Do they advertise on TV, on the radio or in newspapers?

- Are they online?

- Are their products made in your country?

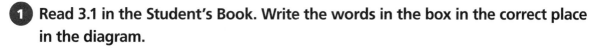

1 Read 3.1 in the Student's Book. Write the words in the box in the correct place in the diagram.

| racial discrimination   negative belief   sexism   personal set of rules |
| a one-sided negative thought   rules for living in society |
| right and wrong   racism   hostility |

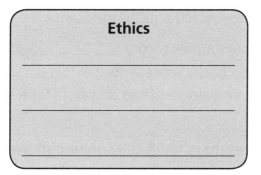

Ethics

_____

_____

_____

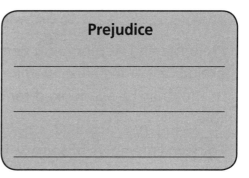

Prejudice

_____

_____

_____

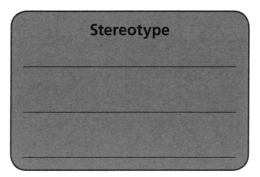

Stereotype

_____

_____

_____

2 Women can sometimes be overlooked for a job in favour of a man. Write an essay about how you think this would affect the relationship between colleagues. Write 200–250 words.

Think about:

- Is this unethical, a prejudice, stereotyping or sexism?

- Or is it a combination of all of them?

- What can be done about it?

3 Read 3.1 in the Student's Book. Complete the statements below.

a) Stereotyping and prejudice can have a _____ impact on society.

b) Examples of this include putting _____ on people as to how they should live their lives according to their _____, sex or religion.

c) Prejudice and stereotyping can cause low _____, emotional problems and _____.

d) Prejudice and stereotyping can allow all prejudices, including _____ and _____, to grow in society, which creates ignorance.

e) Prejudice and stereotyping deny opportunities to the _____ of prejudice. For instance, women can be badly represented in _____, as they may be overlooked for a job, or paid less than a man for the same job role.

f) For some members of society, it makes them more determined to overcome _____ and _____. For example, they work hard to get a good job or education despite people's prejudices.

g) Examples of prejudice on a regional and global scale include:
Hitler's _____ against and _____ of the Jews during World War II.

h) Widespread racial discrimination in some countries – for example, the United States, throughout the _____ trade in the eighteenth and nineteenth centuries, and for some time afterwards; some argue that it is still widespread in the USA.

i) Women not being allowed to _____ in many countries until the twentieth century.

j) Discrimination against sexual _____.

k) In Europe, there is increasing discrimination against _____.

4 Read 3.2 in the Student's Book about the social impact of prejudice and stereotyping, and answer the questions.

a) Where do children and adults generally learn about stereotypes?

_____

b) What forms does this include?

_____

_____

c) What examples of social media are given?

_____

d) What types of stereotypes does the media often portray?

_____

e) What examples can you give of this?

i) _____

ii) _____ ,

girls/women, iii) _____ ;

boys/men, iv) _____

v) _____

vi) _____

f) Name the four basic types of negative stereotyping of women:

i) _____

ii) _____

iii) _____

iv) _____

g) Men are often shown as _____ , with a strong sense of

_____ .

5 **Look at the case study on page 55 in the Student's Book. Read the statements below and write ASA for Advertising Standards Authority or HK for Hurricane Katrina next to each one.**

a) Gender stereotyping of women cleaning _____

b) Decline in race relations _____

c) Evacuees were unable to find refuge locally _____

d) Prospects for young people were affected _____

e) Stronger rules are needed _____

f) Race relations were affected _____

g) Some people were portrayed as criminals _____

h) Someone investigated for a year _____

i) People portrayed as stealing from other people _____

j) Advertisements by certain companies showed stereotypes _____

k) Members of the public complained _____

l) The media focused on certain people _____

6 **Discuss as a class the following questions.**

a) Where do you see advertisements?

b) Why do companies advertise?

c) What do you think of advertisements?

d) Why do you think they are good or bad?

e) Are you influenced by adverts?

f) Which advertisements do you think stereotype women?

7 Read 3.3 in the Student's Book. Answer the questions or complete the statements below.

    a) What is another word for religious prejudice?

    _____

    b) Some people are treated differently because of the _____ that they belong to, or what they believe in.

    c) What is the central principle of most religions?

    _____

    Many religious teachings include:

    d) the understanding that differences between social groups are often caused by differences in **(i)** _____, instead of differences between the people themselves; advocating **(ii)** _____ pluralism, which is a teaching that many different religious belief systems can **(iii)** _____ in the same society and accept that different religions, with different beliefs, can be equally **(iv)** _____; challenging ideologies that are **(v)** _____ against any forms of religion.

    e) What is being encouraged amongst different religious groups?

    _____

    f) What does creating opportunities hope to achieve?

    _____

    g) What did Farid Esack challenge in South Africa?

    _____

    h) What is apartheid?

    _____

8 Read 3.3 in the Student's Book. Match the four largest religious groups' views and beliefs about prejudice and discrimination with the correct religion.

Christianity

a) i) _____

   ii) _____

   iii) _____

Hinduism

b) i) _____

   ii) _____

   iii) _____

All people should get on with one another

The aim of life is moksha

Humans share the same dignity and values as God

Human beings are the highest form of life

Do not let hatred of others lead them to sin

All people should be treated with respect

Prejudice and discrimination are fundamentally wrong

Live a good life

Humans are created in the image of God

Each person is unique

Live a righteous life

All people are equal in the eyes of God

Islam

c) i) _____

   ii) _____

   iii) _____

Judaism

d) i) _____

   ii) _____

   iii) _____

9 **Complete the crossword. All the words are key vocabulary words from 3.1–3.3 in the Student's Book.**

Across

1. The holy book of Islam
3. An unreasonable feeling or opinion, especially the feeling of not liking a particular group of people
5. Behaving in a way traditionally considered typical of a man
7. Respect that other people have for you or that you have for yourself
11. Television, films, radio, adverts, social media (4, 5)
12. To hold a one-sided negative thought or belief about how another person, or a group of people, acts or behaves
13. The treatment of a person or a group of people differently because of the religion that they belong to, or what they believe in (9, 9)
14. The qualities that are thought to be typical of men

Down

2. Prejudice against a race or ethnicity
4. The fact that someone belongs to a particular group of people who have the same culture and traditions
5. To be liberated
6. A group of people who are similar because they speak the same language or have the same history or customs
8. Prejudice against a member of the opposite sex
9. The rules for living in society according to what we consider to be right or wrong
10. A system in South Africa whereby people were kept apart on racial grounds

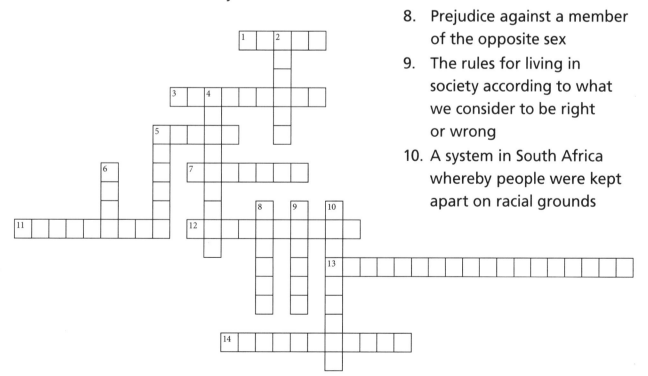

10 **Read 3.4 in the Student's Book. Then read the statements and circle True or False. Then correct the False sentences.**

a) Conflict is a minor disagreement between two or more people.   **True**   **False**

b) Conflict happens through a difference of opinions, views, ideas or needs.
True   **False**

c) Behind every conflict is the need to feel safe, respected, recognised or loved.
True   **False**

d) Conflicts at school are not usually caused by peer pressure or bullying.
True   **False**

e) Peer pressure is when your classmates encourage you to do something you really want to try.   **True**   **False**

f) A bully is a person who uses physical or verbal abuse towards someone else.   **True**   **False**

g) A person being bullied can suffer from several mental health issues, such as depression, anxiety, loneliness or sadness.   **True**   **False**

h) Bullying rarely has any physical effects on the person being bullied.
True   **False**

i) Students being bullied try to avoid school.   **True**   **False**

j) Students being pressured by their peers look forward to going to school.
True   **False**

k) Students who suffer from peer pressure can start drinking alcohol or taking drugs.   **True**   **False**

11 Read 3.4 in the Student's Book. Then unscramble each word and match them with the correct definition.

a) t o c c i f l n   _____

b) c l i f t o c n   n i l o s u t o r e   _____

c) a n t i m e i d o   _____

d) t r o m n e   _____

e) r e p e   s p e r e s u r   _____

f) l y g i n l u b   _____

i)   Try to end a disagreement between two people or groups

ii)   When an individual or group tries to intimidate others through physical or verbal abuse

iii)   When people of the same age try to influence someone to do something they do not want to do

iv)   A serious disagreement or clash between two or more people

v)   Someone who gives advice and help to another person over a period of time

vi)   The process of ending a conflict and finding a peaceful way forward

12 Write approximately 250 words about your mentor. Think about the following:

- Who has helped you the most throughout your life?

- Who has given you good advice?

- Has their help improved your attitude or behaviour?

- Has their advice helped you at school?

- As a result of their help, do you have good communication skills?

13 Find the words listed below in the word search puzzle. These words are from 3.1–3.4 in the Student's Book. The words can be horizontal, diagonal, vertical, backwards or forwards.

peer pressure	Judaism	religious pluralism	mediation	conflict
conflict resolution	Christianity	Islam	bullying	Hinduism	mentor

J	S	N	Z	T	N	X	M	A	N	J	R	H	L	Q	Z	C	H
Q	L	L	M	S	O	R	S	E	U	P	X	Q	E	Y	O	W	D
B	E	R	K	P	I	Y	M	V	D	Z	A	R	T	N	P	C	W
B	S	B	C	C	T	K	R	N	N	I	U	K	F	Y	Y	N	T
E	U	W	R	X	U	J	D	X	J	S	A	L	A	J	Y	E	X
S	Z	F	P	L	L	R	S	L	S	G	I	T	N	Q	M	U	D
L	O	K	A	V	O	P	D	E	O	C	Y	D	I	C	G	T	I
S	Z	U	U	W	S	Y	R	V	T	M	E	Q	L	O	F	L	P
F	E	B	M	T	E	P	M	U	T	B	S	I	B	H	N	U	S
M	S	I	L	A	R	U	L	P	S	U	O	I	G	I	L	E	R
M	R	A	W	E	T	C	H	R	I	S	T	I	A	N	I	T	Y
Q	O	N	E	W	C	C	W	U	X	M	S	E	S	D	Y	W	H
T	W	P	R	B	I	X	Q	E	A	J	S	D	I	U	U	N	U
T	Z	U	O	C	L	M	E	L	S	K	V	O	J	I	G	J	A
H	P	I	T	Q	F	A	S	Y	D	E	X	A	R	S	I	H	J
O	A	E	N	C	N	I	M	E	J	E	Q	Z	O	M	U	M	R
W	X	C	E	A	O	M	I	G	M	Q	S	C	K	T	X	Z	P
A	U	M	M	A	C	G	N	I	Y	L	L	U	B	A	X	U	Z

14 Now write the words in alphabetical order.

a) _____ b) _____

c) _____ d) _____

e) _____ f) _____

g) _____ h) _____

i) _____ j) _____

k) _____

1 Complete the crossword. All the words are key vocabulary words from 4.1 and 4.2 in the Student's Book.

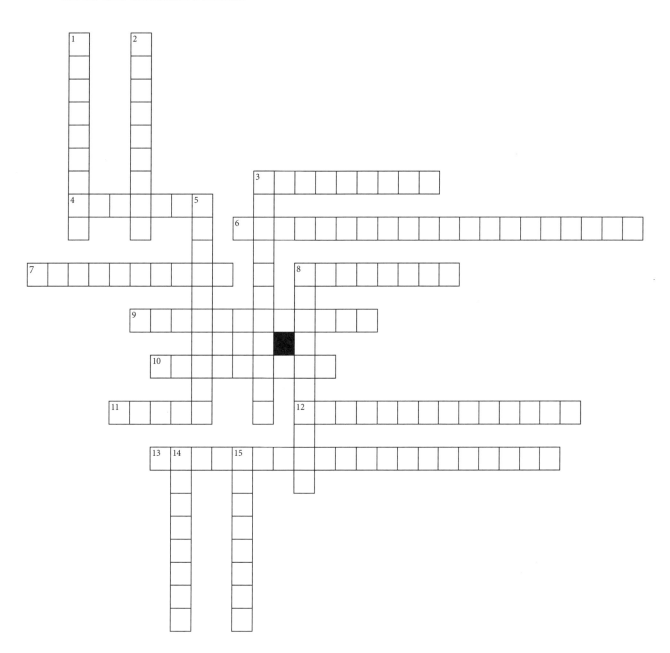

Across

3. A person who seeks to be nominated or elected to a position in the national or local government
4. A person who has the right to vote in an election
6. One of the people competing in an election who is not a member of one of the main political parties (11, 9)
7. People who believe in the ideas of a particular person or group
8. A time to choose people who will serve in local and national government
9. An area of a country that elects a representative to parliament
10. A statement that publicly states what a candidate's views are on certain issues and explains the policies they support or will introduce if they are elected
11. People supporting their choice of a person or an issue in an election
12. A politician who is a member of the government
13. A system whereby people vote for candidates who, if they get enough votes and are elected, serve in the government (10, 10)

Down

1. Officially suggested that someone should stand for parliament
2. A system of government in which people vote in elections to choose the people who will govern them
3. The people who live in an area who vote for who they want to represent them in local and national elections
5. The people who have been voted into parliament
8. All the people in a country who are eligible and registered to vote in an election
14. Allowed by the law to do something
15. A series of events that are organised to help a candidate get elected

2 Read the case study in 4.3 in the Student's Book. Then number the following procedures (1–6) in the order they take place on Nomination Day in Dominica.

_____ **a)** The candidates' deposits are taken to the treasury

_____ **b)** The candidates' information is sent to the Electoral Office

_____ **c)** Each candidate makes a statutory declaration that they are properly qualified to be nominated as a candidate

_____ **d)** The ballot papers are prepared

_____ **e)** Candidates present themselves to returning officers in their respective constituencies with six electors from their constituencies in order to be nominated

_____ **f)** Each candidate makes a deposit of $500 for their nomination

3 Read 4.3 and 4.4 in the Student's Book. Then match each word to the correct definition.

a) ballot paper	**i)** the right that people have to vote in elections
b) nomination	**ii)** to have the right to vote
c) franchise	**iii)** something on which someone records their vote next to the name of a candidate
d) ballot box	**iv)** when people register to stand as a candidate
e) adult suffrage	**v)** this allows people to vote anonymously and freely
f) secret ballot	**vi)** a special place which is sealed so that people cannot tamper with it
g) Nomination Day	**vii)** a vote or a piece of paper on which a person records their vote
h) ballot	**viii)** the procedure candidates have to follow in order to stand for election

4 Read 4.5 and 4.6 in the Student's Book. Then answer the following questions.

a) How often do elections have to be held?

_____

b) Under what circumstances can the Prime Minister, Premier or President, or Chief Minister call for early elections?

_____

c) Who informs voters when elections will be?

_____

d) What is a hung parliament?

_____

e) How many people do candidates have to be nominated by?

_____

f) What information can be found on the poll cards?

_____

g) What do candidates and political parties do after Nomination Day?

_____

h) What typically happens during an election campaign?

_____

5 Read 4.6 and 4.7 in the Student's Book. Then complete the following statements.

a) **Factors that influence a political choice:**

i) _____ means the two sexes sometimes vote differently on different issues.

ii) _____ means voters sometimes follow the candidate from the same ethnic group.

iii) _____ – people respond with feeling to a political party or candidate.

iv) _____ means some parties attract loyal supporters.

v) _____ should have an unbiased approach to the elections.

b) **The process on election day:**

    i)   The voter is given an official _____ .

    ii)   The voter enters a private _____ .

    iii) The _____ are taken to a central place where each ballot is counted in the presence of the candidates.

    iv) When all the votes are counted, the results are announced by the

          _____ .

6 Read the key vocabulary in 4.5–4.8 in the Student's Book. Then unscramble the words and match with the correct definition below.

a) ushoe-ot-shueo gnanvacsis

   _____

b) strif taps het stop

   _____

c) tropponailor natrepoteiners

   _____

d) glintofa stovre

   _____

e) merip rentisim

   _____

    i)   A system of voting in which the number of representatives in government from each political party is based on the number of votes each party receives

    ii)   Involving visits to every house in an area to talk to electors to gain their vote

    iii) A system in which someone wins an election if they receive the most votes, even if they do not receive a majority of the total votes

    iv) The political leader in a country that is governed by a parliament

    v)   Electors who are uncertain who to vote for

7 **Read 4.9–4.11 in the Student's Book. Then answer the questions below.**

a) What principles does universal suffrage follow?

_____

b) What four conditions are required to keep elections free and fair?

i) _____

ii) _____

iii) _____

iv) _____

c) What is in the interest of all political parties to ensure?

_____

d) What does a constitution outline?

i) _____

ii) _____

iii) _____

iv) _____

e) What is constitutional reform?

_____

f) How does constitutional reform usually come about?

_____

g) Explain the significance of constitutional reform.

_____

h) What are the consequences of war?

_____

8 Complete the words using the clues given. All the words are key vocabulary words from 4.9–4.12 in the Student's Book.

a) Give people more control over their life or more power to do something

_ _ _ o _ _ _ e _

b) Try not to keep anything secret

_ _ a _ _ _ _ _ e _ _

c) When a government does not punish people who have committed a particular crime

_ _ n _ _ _ _

d) A system when not all citizens are allowed to vote in an election

_ _ m _ _ e _   _ _ a _ _ _ i _ _

e) The process of changing the constitution

_ _ _ _ t _ _ _ _ i _ _ _ _   _ _ _ o _ _

f) The illegal use of fire to destroy a building

_ _ _ o _

g) An attempt to overthrow the government

_ o _ _   d' _ _ a _

h) Fighting between countries or groups

_ _ _ _ _ l _ _ _

i) When all competent adults in the country have the right to vote

_ _ i _ _ _ _ a _   _ _ _ _ r _ _ e

j) When the parties taking part in an election do not try to persuade citizens to cast their votes in their favour by using force or intimidation

_ _ e _   _ _ d   _ a _ _

9 Read 4.13–4.15 in the Student's Book. Match the words in the box to the correct heading in each circle.

International Tribunal	reunite	multinational
standard of rightness	genocide	humanitarian laws
peacekeeping mission	food and shelter	restore democracy
international criminal court	violated	aid

Peacekeepers
in Haiti

_____
_____
_____

Human dignity

_____
_____
_____

Strategies for
making a difference

_____
_____
_____

The need
for justice

_____
_____
_____

10 Imagine that you are a volunteer for the United Nations High Commission for Refugees (UNHCR). You have been asked to go to another Caribbean island where a conflict has just ended.

Write a letter to a friend telling him or her what supplies you took with you and what you did while you were there to help the people.

Write 200–250 words.

_____

_____

_____

11 Read 4.15–4.17 in the Student's Book. Circle the number of the word or phrase that best completes each sentence.

a) All human beings are born _____ in dignity and rights.

    i) free and fair

    ii) to freedom of movement

    iii) free and equal

    iv) to freedom of thought

b) For minor criminal offences, people can be sentenced to _____.

    i) prison

    ii) punishment

    iii) community service

    iv) a trial

c) The Judiciary ensures that there is equal _____ for all people under the laws of the country.

    i) resolve

    ii) remedy

    iii) conflict

    iv) justice

d) The Supreme Court is made up of the _____ and the High Court.

    i) Court of Appeal

    ii) Magistrates Court

    iii) Family Court

    iv) Court of Justice

e) Justice is served through proper punishment or _____ by the judicial system.

    i) human rights

    ii) fair treatment

    iii) equal access

    iv) treated equally

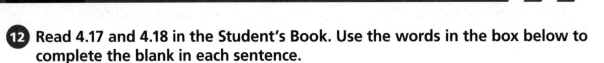

12 **Read 4.17 and 4.18 in the Student's Book. Use the words in the box below to complete the blank in each sentence.**

regional integration	International Criminal Court	dictator
Caribbean Court of Justice	war crimes	crimes against humanity
genocide disputes	justice	international tribunals

a) The _____ has the power to prosecute people all over the world for crimes committed during war.

b) Trinidad and Tobago is referred to as the 'seat' of the

_____.

c) The presence of the Caribbean Court of Justice has helped to further strengthen _____.

d) The ICC in The Hague can prosecute people who have committed _____ anywhere in the world.

e) The ICC is also able to put on trial anyone for

_____.

f) Temporary _____ were set up after the end of World War II.

g) The _____ Pol Pot is said to have killed up to three million people during his reign of terror.

h) Thomas Dyilo was found guilty of _____, including abducting children and using them as soldiers.

i) The CCJ can deal with _____ between member states.

j) The aim of the CCJ is to provide high quality _____ to the people of the Caribbean.

5　Our environment

1　Read 5.1 and 5.2 in the Student's Book. Circle the word or phrase in each group that does not belong with the rest. Say why the item does not belong. On the lines provided, write a sentence using the words/phrases you circled.

a) i)　Fertilisers　_____

  ii)　GM crops　_____

  iii)　Eco-friendly　_____

  iv)　Pesticides　_____

b) i)　Autonomous cars　_____

  ii)　Online　_____

  iii)　Global network　_____

  iv)　Emailing　_____

c) i)　Thatched roof　_____

  ii)　Irrigation equipment　_____

  iii)　Keeping livestock　_____

  iv)　Local materials　_____

d) i)　Bullet trains　_____

  ii)　Electric cars　_____

  iii)　Driverless cars　_____

  iv)　Global network　_____

e) i)　Sprinkler systems　_____

  ii)　Reclaimed bricks　_____

  iii)　Drones　_____

  iv)　Cloned animals　_____

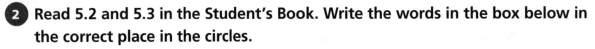

2   **Read 5.2 and 5.3 in the Student's Book. Write the words in the box below in the correct place in the circles.**

use social media sites	destinations	pacemakers
new farming methods	prosthetic limbs	take photos
drone fertilisation	get in touch	inaccessible
remote	precision farming	MRI scanners

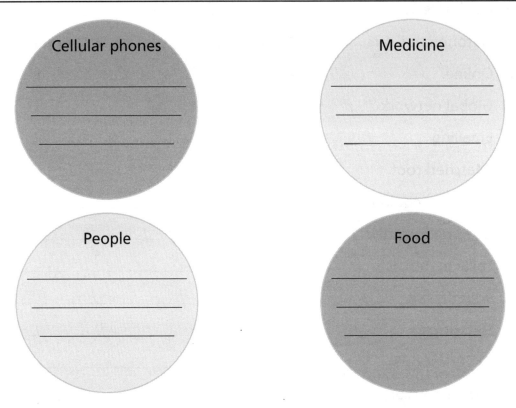

Cellular phones

_____

_____

_____

Medicine

_____

_____

_____

People

_____

_____

_____

Food

_____

_____

_____

3   **Write 200 words on how important your cellular phone is in your personal life. What do you mainly use it for, and how often? Could you live without it?**

_____

_____

_____

_____

_____

4 **Read 5.3 and 5.4 in the Student's Book and then answer the questions below.**

a) Name the four ways people can keep in touch with each other, anywhere in the world.

i) _____   ii) _____

iii) _____   iv) _____

b) Name the three biggest killer diseases in the world today.

i) _____   ii) _____

iii) _____

c) Name the five diseases that are now curable.

i) _____   ii) _____

iii) _____   iv) _____

v) _____

d) What is another expression for spending time looking at an electronic device?

_____

e) What is one cause of obesity?

_____

f) What does using a mobile device or computer do to your body if you use them just before going to bed?

_____

g) What are the two new expressions used to describe aches and pains caused by spending too much time on a computer or mobile device?

i) _____   ii) _____

5 **Do some research and find out which diseases are still deadly in your country. How can people help themselves to prevent these diseases, such as diabetes, and to live longer? Write 250 words.**

Think about:

• What percentage of the population suffers from the disease?

• How many people die from them?

• How could they be prevented?

6 Complete the crossword. All the words are from 5.1–5.3 in the Student's Book.

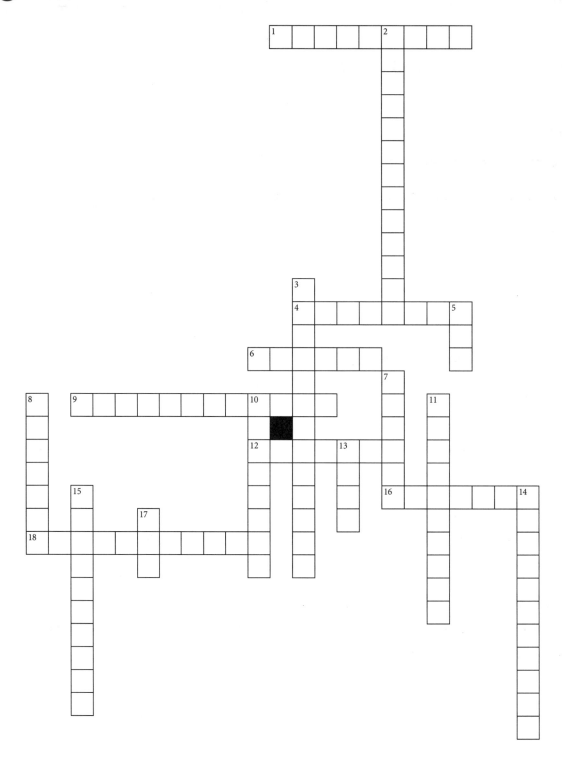

Across

1. Animals such as cows, sheep and pigs that are kept on farms
4. Sending a message to someone using the internet
6. Connected to or available through a computer
9. Difficult or impossible to reach
12. An area of land, usually one with a particular feature
16. The study and knowledge of the physical world based on experiments and facts
18. Capable of continuing for a long time at the same level

Down

2. Related to or involving technology
3. A mobile device (8, 5)
5. A system for finding exactly where you are anywhere in the world
7. Aircraft that do not have a pilot and are controlled from the ground
8. Food that has had its genetic structure changed to make it more suitable for a particular purpose (2, 5)
10. Millions of computers linked together in a network
11. Used to help crops grow
13. Software designed to do a particular job, especially one that people use on a smartphone
14. Designed to cause as little harm to the environment as possible (3–8)
15. Used to kill insects that would damage crops
17. Human immunodeficiency virus

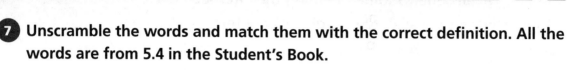
7 **Unscramble the words and match them with the correct definition. All the words are from 5.4 in the Student's Book.**

a) t x t e   b h u m t   _____

b) p l u t o n i o l   _____

c) c r e n e s   e m i t   _____

d) n o z e o   e l r a y   _____

e) s t y e i b o   _____

f) t e a m l i c   g a n c h e   _____

g) t r e d a t o o f e i n s   _____

h) o n h e p   c k e n   _____

i)   A protective layer around the Earth's atmosphere that stops harmful ultraviolet rays from the sun reaching the Earth

ii)   Ache or pain caused by holding a mobile phone to the ear for long periods of time or bending forward to look at a screen

iii) The process of damaging the air, land or water with chemicals or other substances

iv)   The change of the Earth's temperature and weather patterns as a result of increased carbon dioxide in the air

v)   Time spent looking at an electronic device

vi)   When someone is very overweight and it is dangerous for their health

vii) Ache or pain caused by using a mobile device too often to send text messages

viii) The removal of trees and vegetation to create open spaces for human activities

8 Read 5.5 in the Student's Book. Then read the statements and circle True or False.

a) Rural areas do not have as many job opportunities as urban areas do. **True False**

b) Urban areas do not have many employment opportunities. **True False**

c) Subsistence farming gives people enough food to feed themselves and their families. **True False**

d) Many people migrate to urban areas to further their education or find work. **True False**

e) In towns and cities there are more schools and universities available. **True False**

f) Urban areas tend to have more services and amenities for people living there. **True False**

9 Read 5.6 in the Student's Book. Complete the table below with the results of the negative effects of urbanisation.

Negative effects of urbanisation		
Problem	**Effect**	**Result**
Health issues	The movement of people from one area to another can lead to	a) _____ b) Examples: _____ _____
Pollution	Large numbers of vehicles in urban areas, as well as factories, can cause	c) _____ Emission of harmful gases can lead to health problems such as d) _____ _____
Unemployment	People who do not have a job in urban areas can become	e) _____ and turn to f) _____
Shortage of housing	As so many people are attracted to urban areas, there is often not enough	g) _____ This can result in h) _____ _____ being constructed.
Commuting issues	The increasing number of cars on the roads can lead to	i) _____ This situation can also lead to j) _____ in urban areas.
Poverty and crime	A lack of jobs, money and housing can lead people to turn to	k) _____ _____

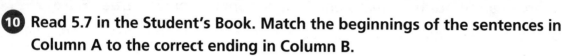
10 Read 5.7 in the Student's Book. Match the beginnings of the sentences in Column A to the correct ending in Column B.

Column A	Column B
a) The average number of people living in a square kilometre	**i)** are frequently overpopulated.
b) Population density is usually	**ii)** offer better facilities in rural areas.
c) Areas or countries with high population densities	**iii)** much higher in urban areas.
d) Overpopulation can cause a number of problems, including	**iv)** some form of contraception.
e) Unemployment can lead to	**v)** difficulty in providing education.
f) One way of controlling population density is	**vi)** is known as the population density of an area.
g) Family planning usually involves	**vii)** to practise family planning.
h) Condoms are the only form of contraception that	**viii)** poverty and perhaps crime.
i) A lack of accommodation can lead to	**ix)** can protect someone from STDs.
j) Another way to control population density is to	**x)** high rents and house prices.
k) Rural–urban migration may take place,	**xi)** due to the distances and terrain involved.
l) Family planning is the practice of controlling the	**xii)** and send in their work to a teacher by the internet.
m) A distance learning course is where the students work at home	**xiii)** number and frequency of children in a family.
n) Electricity supplies in rural areas can be difficult,	**xiv)** which leads to further overcrowding in urban areas.

11 Read 5.7 again. Use the words or expressions in the box to complete each sentence.

distance learning	infrastructure	health centres
initiatives	rainwater	solar power	terrain
diversifying	distribution	wireless	flood	rural

a) Improving the quality of schools in _____ areas can be difficult.

b) _____ suggested to improve education in rural areas include improving the smaller country schools that already exist.

c) Another option to improve education in rural areas is to offer _____ courses via the internet.

d) Supplying water to rural areas is sometimes a problem, as they are a long way from national _____ systems.

e) Solutions to supply rural areas with water include collecting _____, water recycling and the construction of wells.

f) In country areas, roads are often poor quality and prone to _____ or storm damage.

g) Transport _____ would be improved by building better-quality roads from rural to urban areas.

h) Electricity supplies in rural areas can be difficult, partly due to the _____.

i) One solution to improve electricity supplies in rural areas is to generate electricity using local generators operated by _____.

j) Providing _____ communication and internet services to rural areas would help people to connect better to the rest of the world.

k) Government-subsidised health programmes, such as immunisation and _____, would improve health services in rural areas.

l) _____ the economy into other sectors would help create jobs in rural areas.

12 Find the words listed in the word search puzzle below. All the words are from 5.5–5.7 in the Student's Book. The words may be horizontal, vertical or diagonal and may be spelled backwards or forwards. There are 15 words to find.

P	K	V	G	L	S	U	B	S	I	S	T	E	N	C	E	E
U	O	J	D	N	E	H	C	T	L	F	H	J	U	C	D	S
R	T	P	B	X	I	O	A	A	P	I	Z	R	Y	E	U	I
B	N	A	U	X	Y	N	D	N	L	V	B	V	T	R	F	L
A	E	I	I	L	Z	O	N	D	T	A	L	A	R	U	R	A
N	M	R	Y	I	A	S	M	A	N	Y	L	A	Z	O	T	I
I	Y	P	A	R	M	T	G	R	L	U	T	X	B	M	T	R
S	O	O	X	O	N	M	I	D	P	P	K	O	H	X	J	T
A	L	L	K	U	C	I	E	O	F	S	Y	K	W	Z	R	S
T	P	L	D	B	L	G	P	F	N	N	J	L	N	N	Z	U
I	M	U	F	M	R	R	E	L	Y	D	O	U	I	F	Y	D
O	E	T	P	Z	E	A	V	I	U	F	E	V	H	M	L	N
N	N	I	F	V	I	T	W	V	C	N	W	N	E	N	A	I
L	U	O	O	V	G	E	M	I	D	D	M	M	S	R	G	F
B	Z	N	M	Y	N	E	P	N	B	I	O	D	U	I	N	Z
X	S	D	I	M	H	M	Y	G	R	P	E	M	V	L	T	L
T	N	E	M	Y	O	L	P	M	E	R	E	D	N	U	S	Y

13 Now write the words in alphabetical order.

a) _____ b) _____

c) _____ d) _____

e) _____ f) _____

g) _____ h) _____

i) _____ j) _____

k) _____ l) _____

m) _____ n) _____

o) _____

1 Read 6.1 and 6.2 in the Student's Book. Label the diagram below and complete the answers.

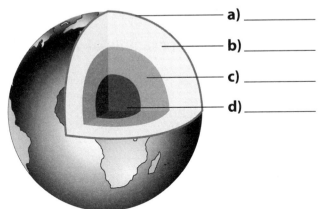

a) _____

b) _____

c) _____

d) _____

e) Name two types of crust.

_____

_____

f) Liquid rock in the mantle is known as _____.

g) The two parts of the core are i) _____ and ii) _____ .

h) The Earth's crust is made up of i) _____ main plates and many more smaller plates. These are called ii) _____ plates.

i) The plates move because they are being pushed and pulled in different directions by _____ inside the mantle.

j) Where two tectonic plates meet it is called a i) _____ or

ii) _____ .

k) _____ (or transform) plate margins is when two plates slide past each other.

l) _____ (or convergent) plate margins is when two plates move towards each other. In this scenario, one plate is made of continental crust and the other of oceanic crust.

2 Read 6.3 and 6.4 in the Student's Book and complete the answers.

a) A country where volcanic islands appear is _____.

b) The _____ are a good example of where fold mountains have formed.

c) _____ has both volcanoes and earthquakes due to convergent plate margins.

d) The San Andreas Fault causes earthquakes because a conservative plate margin means two plates _____ past each other.

e) Cracks in the Earth's crust are called _____.

f) _____ is the downward movement of an oceanic plate underneath a continental plate into the Earth's mantle in certain areas of the world.

g) A series of waves that form in the oceans after an earthquake or underwater volcanic eruption is known as a _____. These waves travel at speeds of more than 950 km per hour.

h) Although there are many types of rock on the Earth's surface, they fall mainly into one of three categories:

   i) _____

   ii) _____

   iii) _____.

i) There are two types of igneous rock:

   i) _____

   ii) _____

These rocks are formed inside the Earth, beneath the surface.

3 Read the key vocabulary in 6.4 and 6.5 in the Student's Book. Then complete the crossword.

Across

8. Rocks that form above the surface of the Earth (9, 4)

9. Sediment glued together by crystals that form a rock

11. Instruments that record the strength of seismic waves

16. Formed under the seas and oceans from sediment (11, 5)

17. Sudden shaking of the Earth's crust

18. Igneous rocks that form inside the Earth (9, 4)

Down

1. Formed by pressure or heat from underneath the surface of the Earth (11, 5)

2. Became solid or made something solid

3. The point directly above the focus on the Earth's surface

4. Formed when magma from the mantle rises to the surface, then cools and hardens (7, 5)

5. The size of an earthquake

6. A means of knowing the size of an earthquake (7, 5)

7. The result of the movement of tectonic plates, such as an earthquake (7, 8)

10. The point at which an earthquake happens underground

12. Relating to earthquakes

13. Levels of energy that travel through the Earth's layers, as the result of an earthquake (7, 5)

14. Sediment laid down or left behind on the ocean floor

15. Carried or moved along into the seas and oceans

4 Read 6.6–6.8 in the Student's Book. Use the words in the box below to complete the blank in each sentence.

mitigation strategy	evacuation plan	landslide
emergency procedures	Action Plan	insurance	disaster supply kit
aftershocks	devastating	mudslide	prone to	sway

a) Most people who can afford it take out _____ against earthquake damage.

b) When people live in areas that can have earthquakes, most schools have an _____ for when an earthquake strikes.

c) The result of the earthquake in Haiti was _____ , with thousands made homeless.

d) Schools and businesses throughout Asia have an _____ if there is the threat of a tsunami.

e) After the main earthquake in Haiti, there were more than 50 _____.

f) A _____ is a plan to reduce the loss of life and property by lessening the impact of disasters.

g) More than 100 tonnes of wet soil moved down the hill in the _____ that happened after the earthquake.

h) In areas that are _____ earthquakes, many people have a disaster supply kit packed and ready for use in the event of a disaster.

i) Many of the roads were blocked because of fallen rocks and debris caused by the _____.

j) People in areas prone to earthquakes and tsunamis are encouraged to have a _____ in their houses and businesses.

k) It is essential to have informed all students or staff about the _____ we have in place.

l) Japanese architects now design buildings that will _____ when there is an earthquake.

5 Read 6.8–6.10 in the Student's Book. Then answer the questions below.

a) Which items are recommended for all classrooms to have to be prepared for an emergency?

i) _____   ii) _____

iii) _____   iv) _____

v) _____   vi) _____

vii) _____   viii) _____

b) When should you not help others in the event of an emergency?

_____

c) Name the three types of volcano.

i) _____   ii) _____

iii) _____

d) Where do shield volcanoes form?

_____

e) Where do composite volcanoes form?

_____

f) How is a composite volcano structured?

i) _____

ii) _____

iii) _____

g) What did the eruption in Soufrière Hills in 2010 lead to?

_____

h) What ripped through the Belham Valley in 2009?

_____

i) What materials can be ejected from a volcano?

i) _____   ii) _____   iii) _____

6 Read 6.10 and 6.11 in the Student's Book. Then match the beginning of the sentences in Column A with the endings in Column B.

<table>
<tr><td colspan="2">Column A</td><td colspan="2">Column B</td></tr>
<tr><td>a)</td><td>Volcanoes frequently emit carbon dioxide,</td><td>i)</td><td>is a highly toxic gas.</td></tr>
<tr><td>b)</td><td>Small emissions of carbon dioxide</td><td>ii)</td><td>one of the deadliest effects of volcanic eruptions.</td></tr>
<tr><td>c)</td><td>Hydrogen sulphide</td><td>iii)</td><td>and ejected from composite volcanoes.</td></tr>
<tr><td>d)</td><td>Pyroclastic flows are</td><td>iv)</td><td>will not harm people.</td></tr>
<tr><td>e)</td><td>Lahars are fast-moving flows of water and volcanic debris</td><td>v)</td><td>which can lead to headaches and dizziness.</td></tr>
<tr><td>f)</td><td>High viscosity lava is very thick</td><td>vi)</td><td>that can completely bury buildings and roads.</td></tr>
<tr><td>g)</td><td>Large amounts of gas and dust in the atmosphere</td><td>vii)</td><td>it can cause it to stall and crash.</td></tr>
<tr><td>h)</td><td>If ash gets into a plane's engine,</td><td>viii)</td><td>can stop sunlight getting through to the Earth's surface.</td></tr>
</table>

7 Imagine that you are in charge of disaster response after an earthquake or a volcanic eruption. Identify the four activities you would complete first as a priority. Write 250 words.

Think about:

- setting up temporary hospitals
- feeding the homeless and hungry
- restoring the telephone system and electricity
- getting the TV stations running again
- rescuing everyone
- distributing drinking water
- repairing roads, ports and airports to reopen them, or opening schools.

Add any ideas of your own.

8 Read the key vocabulary in 6.12 and 6.13 in the Student's Book. Then unscramble the words and match them to the correct definition.

a) c r e p i n t a p o i t i _____

b) o t h e r g l a m e   g y e r n e _____

c) t h a w e r e _____

d) p r e m a t u r e t e _____

e) f l e t i r e _____

f) d r a s t a u e t _____

g) m e a t l i c _____

h) t h i y u m d i _____

i) i r a   e r r u p e s s _____

j) s t e m e n l e   f o   t h a w e r e _____

i) Soil that is rich in nutrients, so plants grow very well

ii) A pattern of weather in a place over a longer period

iii) A set of conditions in the atmosphere at a particular time and place

iv) The weight of the Earth's atmosphere on the surface

v) The measure of heat energy in the atmosphere around the Earth

vi) Rainfall

vii) When air holds the maximum amount of water vapour possible

viii) The measure of how much water vapour is in the air at any given time

ix) Water that is heated underground and produces steam and can be used to generate electricity

x) Made up of temperature, precipitation, wind, sunshine, cloudiness, humidity and air pressure

9 Read 6.14–6.16 in the Student's Book. Use the words in the box below to complete the blank in each sentence.

rainfall statistics	temperate	mosquitoes
frostbite	rainfall	desert regions	crop
humid	precipitation	isohyet	range of temperatures

a) In tropical areas, temperatures are hot and _____.

b) _____ and temperatures can easily be shown and recorded on a climate graph.

c) Wearing the wrong clothing in a cold country can mean you will suffer from _____.

d) It is important to discover what the _____ is across the whole year before making a climate graph.

e) _____ have less than 250 mm of rainfall a year.

f) _____ growing is highly dependent on the weather and climate.

g) _____ is more likely to fall as snow rather than rain in tundra regions.

h) _____ are found all over the world and not all of them are harmful.

i) _____ maps are maps that are used to show rainfall figures.

j) The most common type of climate graph shows the temperature and _____ over a one-year period.

k) Some of the best regions to farm are in _____ areas, where there are no extreme weather conditions.

10 Read the key vocabulary in 6.15–6.17 in the Student's Book. Then complete the words using the clues given.

a) A violent storm with extremely strong winds and heavy rain

_ _ _ _ i _ _ _ e

b) The centre of a storm

_ y _

c) Information that shows temperature and rainfall statistics for a country or area over a period of time

_ _ _ _ a _ _   _ r _ _ _ s

d) A tropical storm often seen in East Asia

_ _ p _ _ _ _

e) Changes into liquid and forms thick clouds

_ o _ _ e _ _ _ _

f) An area of extreme low pressure

_ i _ _ _ - _ i _ _ _

g) Information that is used to show rainfall figures

_ _ o _ _ _ _   _ _ _ s

h) Change into gas or steam

_ _ a _ _ _ a _ _ _ _

i) The variation of temperatures over a year

_ _ n _ _

j) A severe storm often seen in Southeast Asian countries, such as India and Bangladesh

_ _ _ l _ _ e

11 Read 6.19–6.21 in the Student's Book. Then write the words in the box in the correct place in the diagram.

rain begins   huge storm clouds form   storm surges   air pressure rises early warning and detection   temperatures are higher loss of life and property   winds reach their strongest force   there is no rain disaster supply kits   air pressure starts to fall   winds die down rain turns to showers   flooding   temperatures fall huge, thick clouds form   it is sunny   hurricane shelters   cloud breaks up torrential rain falls   winds increase

Before a hurricane
_____
_____
_____

During a hurricane: the eye-wall
_____
_____
_____

During a hurricane: the eye
_____
_____
_____

During a hurricane: the second eye-wall
_____
_____
_____

After a hurricane
_____
_____
_____

The effects of hurricanes
_____
_____
_____

Preparing for a hurricane
_____
_____
_____

1 Read 7.1 in the Student's Book. Then answer the questions below.

a) What is the expression for when countries in an area cooperate and work together towards common goals?

_____

b) What does integration aim to do for groups of varying backgrounds?

_____

c) What is it called when people of different cultural backgrounds learn tolerance and respect for each other?

_____

d) What is the definition of racial integration?

_____

e) How is economic integration achieved?

_____

f) What is a country's economy made up of?

_____

g) What does cooperation mean?

_____

h) Why does dependence on other people have so many disadvantages?

_____

i) From the 1950s onwards, what did some Caribbean countries start to establish among themselves?

_____

j) What did leaders of Caribbean states see as the way forward to help develop their countries in the Caribbean region?

_____

2 Read 7.2 and 7.3 in the Student's Book. Then answer the questions below.

a) What did ten Caribbean countries form in 1958?

_____

b) What was this the first example of in the region?

_____

c) What word refers to an organisation that has business interests in more than one country?

_____

d) What was the primary intention of the West Indian Federation?

_____

e) What happened to the West Indian Federation in 1962?

_____

f) What was held in Jamaica in September 1961?

_____

g) Who were the two largest countries in the West Indian Federation?

_____

h) What did the member countries of the Federation disagree about?

_____

i) What did the smaller countries of the Federation fear?

_____

j) What was signed in 1965?

_____

k) What was formed from signing this agreement?

_____

3 Read 7.3–7.5 in the Student's Book. Then read the statements below and write CARIFTA, CARICOM, CSME or OECS next to each one.

a) Formed to promote unity and solidarity amongst its members

_____

b) One economic objective is expansion of trade and economic relations with other states _____

c) Promotes cooperation and integration between member states, especially in areas like trade and transportation _____

d) Member states buy and sell more goods amongst themselves

_____

e) Trade between member states was liberalised _____

f) Free movement of money and skilled labour between member states

_____

g) People can move around freely to study and to look for work

_____

h) Anguilla, the British Virgin Islands and Montserrat are associate members

_____

i) A main economic objective is increased production and productivity

_____

j) They can respond as a group to the challenges of opportunities of globalisation _____

k) To make sure there was fair competition, especially for smaller businesses

_____

l) This organisation coordinates foreign policy _____

m) An inter-governmental organisation _____

n) It gives increased cooperation of common services and activities

_____

4 Read 7.5 and 7.6 in the Student's Book. Then complete the statements below.

a) The five sections of OECS are:

i) _____

leads on policy and makes decisions on all matters related to the OECS; made up of the heads of government from each country

ii) _____

implements the policies made by the Authority

iii) _____

reviews legislation passed by the Authority

iv) _____

helps to develop close working relationships with all member countries

v) _____

the administrative part of the organisation

b) The five objectives of the ACS are:

i) _____ _____ _____

of the Caribbean Sea – to ensure that the region as a natural resource is protected for future generations

ii) _____ _____

– protecting the environment, while developing long-term economic opportunities

iii) to develop _____ _____ between the nations

iv) _____ _____ – to develop and put measures in place that will help protect countries and their economies in the event of a natural disaster (such as a hurricane)

v) _____ – better air and sea routes between the member states

5 Read 7.7–7.9 in the Student's Book. Then write the words in the box in the correct place in the circles.

Carifesta	occupational health
autonomous	environmental management
cultural bonds	international tournaments
University of West Indies	Windies diversity
CARICOM countries	research facilities
Caribbean Environmental Health Institute	

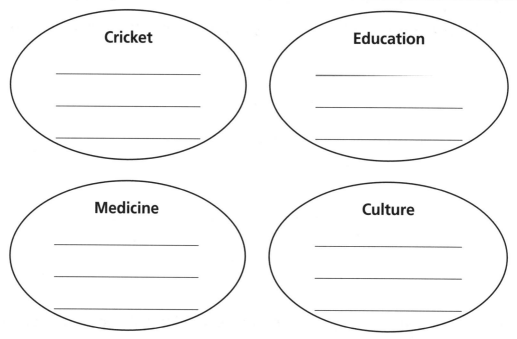

Cricket

Education

Medicine

Culture

6 Choose one of the athletes or cricketers listed on page 186 of the Student's Book and research and write their biography. Write 250 words.

Think about:

- where they were born
- how old they were when they took up their sport
- who encouraged them to be an athlete/cricketer
- which country they represented

- their career statistics
- if they have retired, how old they were when they retired and what they are doing now
- their personal life.

Add any pictures you can find of your chosen athlete/cricketer.

7 Read 7.9–7.11 in the Student's Book. Use the words in the box below to complete the blank in each sentence.

unemployment	earnings	regional market	legislation
prosperity	reliable information	traditions	hurricanes
family duties	global scale	employment	combat crime

a) Citizens share _____, such as washing and cleaning, and looking after family members.

b) _____ is a big problem across the whole of the Caribbean region.

c) Steady economic growth and _____ mean that there is more money available for social programmes, such as better housing, health care, sanitation.

d) CDEMA (the Caribbean Disaster Emergency Management Agency) was set up to coordinate responses to natural disasters such as _____, volcanoes, earthquakes and tsunamis in CARICOM member states and associate member states.

e) Regional integration offers greater opportunities for the Caribbean region to compete on a _____.

f) One of the responsibilities of the Caribbean Disaster Emergency Management Agency is getting _____ after a disaster.

g) Regional integration helps member states to _____ through the Regional Security Service.

h) Retaining a strong _____ also means that the region does not need to rely on global markets in times of global economic difficulty.

i) Increased competition can help to raise _____ and boost sales outside the region, which in turn increases _____ and improves living standards.

j) The role of government includes making sure that _____ works across the region.

k) One of the aims of Carifesta is to depict the myths and _____ of the region.

8 Complete the crossword. All the words are words from 7.5–7.10 in the Student's Book.

Across

2. A particular place or group of people that a product is sold to
4. Something that happens in nature and causes damage or kills many people (7, 8)
5. The qualities that make someone or something what they are and different from other people
11. Capable of continuing having visitors for a long time at the same level (11, 7)
13. The careful use of something so that it is not lost or destroyed
14. Money or property that can be used to start or invest in a business
15. Items that someone owns that can be moved from one place to another
16. Combining things, people or ideas into one effective unit, group or system
17. Conditions and processes relating to people's health, especially the systems that supply water and deal with human waste
18. Freedom from control by another country
19. The workers in a country, industry or company

Down

1. A government department
3. Something that gives people a reason to love one another or feel they have a duty to each other because of what they have in common (8, 5)
6. A situation in which people, groups or countries join together or agree about something
7. A celebration showing the similarities and differences among different groups of people (8, 8)
8. Able to attend certain meetings (8, 6)
9. A group of people or a country that is not allowed to take part in all of another group's activities (9, 6)
10. To make a situation or state continue without changing
12. An arrangement between two or more countries on trade between them (5, 9)
16. Involving governments of different countries (5–12)

9 Read 7.11–7.13 in the Student's Book. Then join the beginnings of the sentences in Column A with the correct ending in Column B.

Column A	Column B
a) Businesses often need investment to	i) raise employment and boost sales.
b) Increased competition can help to	ii) legislation works across the region.
c) The role of government includes making sure that	iii) expand or bring in new equipment.
d) Substance abuse can cause both	iv) drugs and crime in the Caribbean.
e) Gangs are often associated with	v) long- and short-term health problems.
f) A way to combat crime is to	vi) but the effects of the disease can be treated.
g) There is no cure for HIV/AIDS at the moment,	vii) is cuts in government spending.
h) One reason for high unemployment	viii) make sure that crimes are punished fairly.
i) The role of businesses in regional integration includes	ix) enough money to live a comfortable life.
j) Multinational companies are large companies that are	x) better education and training, and increasing economic growth.
k) Poverty is the state of being poor and not having	xi) based in different countries in the region, and often produce a number of different products.
l) Strategies to combat poverty include	xii) increasing the range of goods and services.

10 Read 7.13 and 7.14 in the Student's Book. Then use the words in the box to complete each sentence.

reusing	international partners	terrorism	smog	sewage plants
volatile economies	reducing	recycling	pollution	poverty

a) _____ means not having enough money to live a comfortable life.

b) People being poor in the Caribbean is partly due to _____ constantly changing throughout the region.

c) _____, which can sometimes be found in large towns and cities, can cause asthma and respiratory problems.

d) Air, water, land and noise _____ are all problems in the region.

e) Governments need to provide more places where the public can take items for _____, such as plastic and glass bottles, cans and paper.

f) Many companies need to consider _____ the amount of packaging they put on their products.

g) _____ packaging material is also an option, especially through recycling.

h) The building and maintaining of new _____ is now a priority in the Caribbean region.

i) _____, which is the use of violence to achieve political aims, is a growing problem throughout the world.

j) Countries in the Caribbean work closely with _____ in strategic areas, such as intelligence and information sharing.

11 Read 7.11–7.14 in the Student's Book. Then find the words in the puzzle below. The words can be vertical, horizontal or diagonal and backwards or forwards. There are 16 words to find.

O	D	G	C	I	V	S	I	F	B	C	X	J	K	T
T	R	E	A	R	M	K	G	L	O	Q	W	I	A	S
R	E	X	Y	N	T	N	E	M	T	S	E	V	N	I
E	D	R	Y	O	G	S	P	F	H	I	P	J	N	R
M	U	K	R	N	L	E	G	M	I	O	U	O	Y	O
I	C	V	Y	O	T	P	R	U	V	T	I	E	R	R
R	I	F	D	I	R	G	M	E	R	T	E	A	C	R
C	N	N	T	B	F	I	R	E	U	D	C	G	C	E
S	G	I	A	G	C	T	S	L	N	S	M	O	G	T
Z	O	N	C	P	Y	P	L	M	N	U	R	H	O	Y
N	V	Y	M	S	S	O	G	N	I	S	U	E	R	H
R	F	A	Y	D	P	R	E	C	Y	C	L	I	N	G
D	S	Y	I	F	K	A	C	V	P	Q	S	R	G	F
U	F	A	N	E	V	Q	Z	Y	J	U	K	F	E	B
Z	M	I	O	R	C	Y	Q	U	A	V	N	Z	I	L

Write the words in alphabetical order.

a) _____

b) _____

c) _____

d) _____

e) _____

f) _____

g) _____

h) _____

i) _____

j) _____

k) _____

l) _____

m) _____

n) _____

o) _____

p) _____

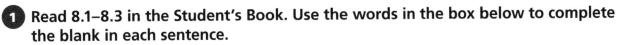
1 **Read 8.1–8.3 in the Student's Book. Use the words in the box below to complete the blank in each sentence.**

primary	unemployment	secondary	standard of living
	self-esteem	tertiary	income	taxes
	technology	employment	employee	

a) Income that helps to provide for our needs and wants also helps to improve our _____.

b) In some industries, new technologies can replace particular job roles. This can cause _____.

c) Working people pay _____. This money helps to provide the goods and services that the whole community needs.

d) Remember, _____ workers extract or harvest resources – for example, farmers, fishermen, miners.

e) _____ workers process or manufacture products, such as factory workers or builders.

f) _____ workers provide services, like doctors, teachers or advertisers.

g) The development of _____ has created many new jobs – from computer programmers, software developers and technicians, to people who run successful businesses using digital technology, social media and the internet.

h) An _____ provides money to pay for everyday living, such as food, clothing and shelter, and can also help to improve our lives.

i) _____ is the state of having work to do. The average _____ stays in the same job for around three to five years.

j) Being a productive part of the wider economy provides _____ for the individual.

2 Read the key vocabulary in 8.1 and 8.2 in the Student's Book. Then unscramble the words below and match them to the correct definition.

a) p l u m m e t o n n e y   _____

b) s q u i l i f t a c i a n o   _____

c) f l e s - s m e e t e   _____

d) e c h o i c   _____

e) s t a w n   _____

f) d r a n s d a t f o g l i n v i   _____

g) g n e w d o k l e   _____

h) r e c a r e   _____

i) l i l s k s   _____

j) s e n d e   _____

i)   How you feel about yourself

ii)   The understanding someone has about a particular subject

iii)   To choose from a range of things

iv)   Things that are essential for everyday living

v)   When someone does not have a job

vi)   Something, such as degrees or diplomas, that you get when you successfully finish a course of study

vii)   Items that a person would like to have, but are not essential for everyday life or basic survival

viii)   The level of comfort and wealth that a person or family may have

ix)   A person's long-term path in a job or occupation

x)   To have the ability, creativity or knowledge to do something well

3 **Read 8.4 in the Student's Book. Then answer the questions below.**

a) What does a hotelier do?

_____

b) What do some bigger hotels have?

_____

c) What do events planners organise?

i) _____   ii) _____

iii) _____   iv) _____

d) What are the functions of the marketing staff in a hotel?

_____

e) What are the main duties of the housekeeping staff?

_____

f) Apart from welcoming new guests, what else do the reception staff do?

i) _____

ii) _____

g) Who may the kitchen staff include?

i) _____   ii) _____

iii) _____   iv) _____

v) _____

h) What do tour guides do?

_____

i) What does a caterer organise with a client?

i) _____

ii) _____

j) What did Philip do after finishing his training?

_____

4 Read 8.5 in the Student's Book. Then answer the questions below.

a) What do people bring to their work?

   i) _____   **ii)** _____

   iii) _____   **iv)** _____

   v) _____

b) What is the definition of knowledge?

_____

c) What is a skill?

_____

_____

d) How do we develop our skills?

_____

e) What personal qualities should be taken into account to decide on a career?

   i) _____   **ii)** _____

   iii) _____

f) What academic capabilities should be considered before deciding on a career path?

   i) _____

   ii) _____

g) What might happen to a weaker student in the future if they studied something that really interested them?

_____

h) Research the names and types of institutions in your country that offer training after graduating from secondary school.

_____

_____

5 Read 8.5–8.7 in the Student's Book. Then write the words in the box in the correct place in the diagram.

cooperation	shift work	references	needs and wants
experience	scholarship	education	values and attitudes
opportunities for promotion		teacher training college	curriculum
interests and hobbies	health issues	universities	problem solving
contact information	potential	nursing school	passion talents

Qualifications
_____
_____
_____
_____
_____

Institutions
_____
_____
_____
_____

**Questions to consider
when choosing a career**
_____
_____
_____
_____

**Other factors to consider
when choosing a career**
_____
_____
_____
_____

Elements of a résumé
_____
_____
_____
_____

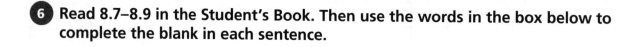

6 **Read 8.7–8.9 in the Student's Book. Then use the words in the box below to complete the blank in each sentence.**

intimate relationship	scholar	communicate
résumé	enemies	suggestive
take responsibility	respectful	hierarchy
workplace relationships	innovative	

a) A _____ should include key information, including a summary of what you can offer the employer.

b) He is a distinguished _____ , who used to attend this school.

c) The new science teacher uses very _____ methods to make the subject interesting.

d) Some _____ require people to work hard to show politeness and to develop a sense of connection to each other.

e) The _____ of an office means that workers can get into conflicts with colleagues.

f) Some work friendships can develop into an _____, though most employers discourage this.

g) Having _____ at work can badly damage the cohesion of the group, and can reduce the job satisfaction of the people involved.

h) It's always best to be friendly, professional and _____ towards your work colleagues.

i) It is important to _____ clearly and politely with your co-workers, answer all letters and emails and return calls.

j) Workers have to _____ and should always try to carry through with what they said they would do.

k) Marianne complained about a co-worker after he had made _____ remarks to her.

7 Read the key vocabulary in 8.5–8.8 in the Student's Book. Then find the words in the word search puzzle. The words can be horizontal, diagonal, vertical, backwards or forwards. There are 10 words to find.

T	N	D	C	U	R	R	I	C	U	L	U	M	Q	N	X	Q	T	Q	W
R	N	U	K	K	E	I	O	X	N	G	C	G	E	T	A	C	O	W	W
H	I	R	J	L	Q	I	X	I	R	E	P	P	F	A	C	E	C	T	I
A	A	O	Q	B	N	T	T	D	U	S	Q	M	T	U	G	Z	O	E	P
P	G	V	O	U	T	I	Z	F	P	I	V	Q	Q	L	Y	T	N	R	B
D	O	X	W	J	F	Q	R	O	E	X	V	F	C	U	J	X	T	I	D
Q	J	D	W	U	S	E	N	T	R	E	P	R	E	N	E	U	R	A	L
Y	H	H	M	N	M	U	O	P	M	K	N	Q	Q	C	O	T	A	Q	N
Y	R	R	E	I	X	B	T	I	A	F	M	S	E	Z	P	J	C	I	L
I	A	A	O	O	S	V	B	O	N	N	Z	H	T	K	F	U	T	L	Q
V	P	K	T	R	M	P	H	I	E	E	R	S	Y	P	T	L	W	B	S
U	G	U	S	N	A	Z	B	I	N	V	O	S	H	C	K	J	O	A	R
H	J	Y	Y	U	U	M	F	F	T	Q	I	L	C	J	S	L	R	O	J
M	M	U	V	E	X	L	O	U	N	J	N	A	R	R	H	G	K	Z	U
B	H	W	E	N	D	R	O	O	M	D	E	U	A	N	W	U	Y	L	N
O	D	Q	J	D	M	N	I	V	Q	E	S	Q	R	Q	W	V	V	M	B
X	U	J	H	A	F	S	M	E	N	E	W	E	E	I	B	H	V	O	W
V	A	V	L	U	S	O	D	C	P	I	R	Q	I	N	F	V	Q	B	G
L	H	M	H	A	B	R	R	E	T	O	N	A	H	F	Q	G	X	T	L
G	E	P	P	T	J	B	L	R	D	C	I	C	O	A	A	I	N	M	J

8 Now write the words in alphabetical order.

a) _____   b) _____

c) _____   d) _____

e) _____   f) _____

g) _____   h) _____

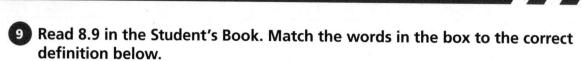

8   Personal development (cont.)

9 Read 8.9 in the Student's Book. Match the words in the box to the correct definition below.

unsolicited	sexual harassment	obscene
innuendoes	suggestive	inappropriate

a) _____

behaviour towards someone of a flirting or sexual nature that the person has not encouraged

b) _____

the use of statements with a possible second meaning, usually referring to sex and intended as a joke

c) _____

any unwanted gesture or communication that has a sexual content

d) _____

remarks of a sexual nature

e) _____

offensive in a sexual way

f) _____

not suitable in a particular situation, especially the workplace

10 What will you expect from a job in the future? Write what is important or unimportant to you about your future career. Write 250 words.

Think about:

- the salary
- working hours
- flexible working hours
- working from home
- friendly colleagues
- chances of promotion

- annual increase in salary
- sexual harassment rules
- dangerous conditions
- continuous training
- any of your own ideas.

11 Read 8.11 and 8.12 in the Student's Book. Answer the following questions about the workplace.

a) If a dispute between employers and employees cannot be settled, and the employees are members of a trade union, who can mediate?

  i)   The local magistrates court

  ii) The government

  iii) An independent court

  iv) The trade union

b) What is the main benefit of belonging to a trade union?

  i)   Building solidarity

  ii) It looks after its members

  iii) Collective bargaining

  iv) Housing assistance

c) What is it called when workers deliberately reduce their work rate?

  i)   Work to rule

  ii) Go on strike

  iii) Stay away from work

  iv) Go slow

d) If someone has a grievance against another employee, what does a company normally start?

  i)   Internal procedures

  ii) Informal discussions

  iii) Independent decisions

  iv) Impartial solutions

e) Collective bargaining is for all a trade union's members. **True   False**

f) Being a member of a trade union can help provide job security. **True   False**

g) The National Workers Union in St Lucia represents 50,000 workers. **True   False**

h) The aims of the Barbados Union of Teachers (BUT) include raising concerns about health and safety of teachers and students in schools. **True   False**

12 **Read the key vocabulary in 8.11 and 8.12 in the Student's Book. Then complete the words using the clues given.**

a) A disagreement between workers and their employer

_ _ _ u _ _ _ i _ _   _ _ _ _ _ _ _ e

b) Organisations of working people, such as trade unions, that campaigned for better conditions

_ a _ _ _ _   _ o _ e _ _ _ _

c) When workers do just enough work so they are within the terms of their job role or contract

_ o _ _   _ _ _   _ u _ _

d) Discussions between employers and trade unions about pay and working conditions

_ _ _ _ e _ _ _ _ e   _ a _ _ a _ _ _ _ _

e) Try to end a disagreement between two people or groups

_ _ _ i _ _ _

f) State formally that you are leaving a job permanently

_ _ s _ _ _ _

g) When workers do not work so fast

_ _   _ _ o _

h) An organisation of workers that aims to improve pay and conditions for its members

_ r _ _ _ _   _ _ i _ _

13 **Should everybody have a right to strike? Or should employers have the right to fire employees who choose not to work? Write 250 words.**

_____

_____

_____

_____

_____

9   History of the Eastern Caribbean

1   **Read 9.1 and 9.2 in the Student's Book. Then answer the questions.**

a) How long ago did the Amerindians settle in the Caribbean?

_____

b) Where did these settlers originally come from?

_____

c) What were the names of the two tribes that arrived from Venezuela?

_____

d) What was the population of the islands at the time Columbus arrived in 1492?

_____

e) What did the indigenous Amerindians grow?

   i) _____   ii) _____

   iii) _____   iv) _____

   v) _____   vi) _____

   vii) _____   viii) _____

f) What else did they eat?

_____

g) What artefacts have been found by archaeologists?

   i) _____   ii) _____

   iii) _____

h) Where in the Caribbean have clay anvils, stone axes and shell axes been found?

_____

i) What was the name of the tribe who settled on St Vincent?

_____

2 **Read 9.3 and 9.4 in the Student's Book. Then answer the questions.**

a) Who were the first European settlers to arrive in the Caribbean?

_____

b) Which islands did these first Europeans settle in?

_____

c) Which nations followed the first European settlers into the Caribbean?

_____

d) In which year did the French settle in Grenada?

_____

e) What factors caused the Amerindian population to decrease in the period up to 1800?

_____

f) Where in the Caribbean today can descendants of the Amerindians still be found?

_____

g) Who took over the occupation of Tobago in 1793?

_____

h) In your own words, describe the events in 1650 on Grenada.

_____

_____

_____

_____

_____

_____

_____

3 Read 9.5 and 9.6 in the Student's Book. Use the words in the box below to complete the blank in each sentence.

Representative	peasant	property	Crown Colony
Legislative Council		Spanish	metayage
Assembly	British	apprenticeships	

a) In establishing its colonies in the Caribbean the British implemented the _____ system of government.

b) Through this system the colonies were ruled by a Governor, Legislative Council and an _____.

c) The _____ was nominated by the Governor from prominent planters and merchants in the colonies.

d) A person's ability to vote was dependent on ownership of _____.

e) By the mid-1860s the British system of control of Caribbean islands was changed to _____ Government.

f) Roman Catholicism was introduced to the Caribbean region by the _____ and the French.

g) Protestant denominations, such as Anglicanism, Methodism and Presbyterianism were introduced to the Caribbean by the _____.

h) _____ were for ex-slaves who had to serve their former owners free of charge for 40.5 hours a week for 4 to 6 years.

i) The small-scale rearing of livestock, growing of vegetables and ground provisions is known as _____ farming.

j) The _____ system was a form of sharecropping where the sharecropper occupied a piece of land on which he or she planted cane.

4 Read the key vocabulary in 9.1–9.6 in the Student's Book. Then complete the crossword.

Across

2. Being freed from slavery
4. The first known population of a place, usually indigenous people (5, 6)
5. Originally present in a place
9. An object that is historically or culturally interesting
12. Statue or building erected in commemoration of a person or event
13. A form of sharecropping (8, 6)
14. A Protestant denomination that follows a 'middle way' between Catholicism and Protestantism
15. One of the world's oldest religions, originally from India
16. To swear loyalty or commitment to someone or something (4, 2, 10)
17. A Protestant denomination based on the teachings of John Wesley

Down

1. Another name for Arawak, indigenous people of the Caribbean
3. The small-scale rearing of livestock and growing of vegetables (7, 7)
6. When someone works for someone else to learn a skill
7. A branch of Christianity
8. Another name for Carib, indigenous people of the Caribbean
10. A group having a distinctive interpretation of Christianity
11. A religion that originated in what is now Saudi Arabia

5 Read 9.6 and 9.7 in the Student's Book. Then match the beginnings of the sentences in Column A with the endings in Column B.

Column A	Column B
a) Sugar was the most prominent crop grown in the Caribbean.	**i)** were given full emancipation.
b) The ex-slaves preferred to use land for	**ii)** to keep sugar estates going.
c) The plantation owners then introduced an	**iii)** other types of farming.
d) All slaves in the British West Indies	**iv)** setting up their own small businesses.
e) The start of peasant farming saw ex-slaves	**v)** respect and the freedom to protest if necessary.
f) The metayage system was developed in order	**vi)** It was often referred to as King Sugar.
g) In the 1920s and 1930s, workers wanted better working conditions,	**vii)** apprenticeship system.
h) Barbados attained universal adult suffrage in 1950,	**viii)** the development of trade unions and political parties.
i) Social activism and social justice led to	**ix)** and Grenada followed in 1951.

6 Read 9.7 and 9.8 in the Student's Book. Then complete the words using the clues given.

a) The set of systems in a country that affects how well it operates, such as roads and communications

_ _ _ r _ _ _ _ u _ _ _ _ e

b) Certain requirements that must be met before being able to vote in an election, e.g. must own property or be over a certain age

_ i _ _ _ e _   _ _ _ n _ _ i _ _

c) Bring about changes and influence the government

_ _ _ i _ _   _ _ t _ _ i _ _

d) All people of a certain age who have the right to vote in an election

_ _ _ _ t   _ _ _ _ _ r _ _ e

e) A system of government in which people vote in elections to choose the people who will govern them

_ _ _ o _ _ a _ _

f) Fair and proper administration of laws conforming to the idea that all persons, irrespective of ethnic origin, gender, possessions, race, religion, etc., are to be treated equally and without prejudice

_ _ c _ _ _ _   _ _ _ _ _ _ c _

g) A system whereby each person over the age of 18 has the right to vote

_ ni _ er _ _ l   _ d _ _ t   _ uf _ _ ag _

h) A system of government that was free from British rule

_ e l _ - g _ _ er _ in _

i) An association of workers that acts on behalf of a group of workers

_ r _ _ e   _ ni _ _

j) A system of government in which a country's citizens choose their rulers by voting for them in elections

_ e _ oc _ ac _

7 Read 9.8–9.10 in the Student's Book. Then write the words below in the correct place in the diagram.

Legislative Council, Grenada	Antigua Labour Party	education for girls

Dominica Labour Party   St Kitts and Nevis Trades and Labour Union

scholarship   female minister   better wages for workers

holidays with pay   newspaper editor

First National Hero   West Indies Federation

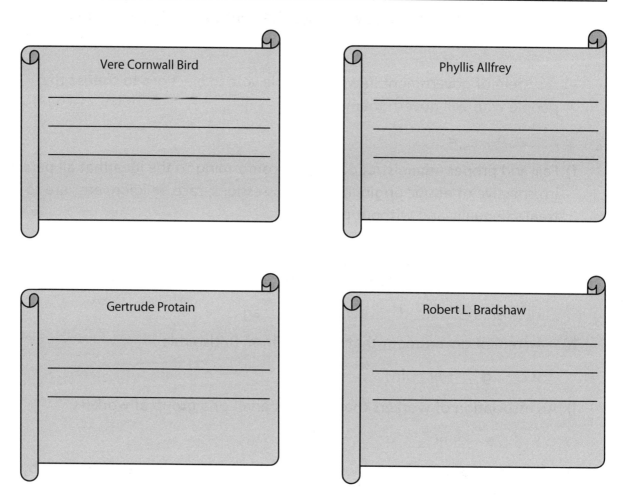

Vere Cornwall Bird

Phyllis Allfrey

Gertrude Protain

Robert L. Bradshaw

8 Read 9.11–9.14 in the Student's Book. Use the words in the box below to complete the blank in each sentence.

Black Power Movement	Civil Rights Movement	Independence
Unity referendum	patriotism	Trinidad and Tobago
Barbados	1974 1979	1978

a) The _____ took hold across the Caribbean, in particular Trinidad and Tobago.

b) Trinidadians were also influenced by the American _____, who wanted to end discrimination against African Americans.

c) The West Indian Federation wanted to achieve _____ from Britain and they saw regional _____ as a way to do this.

d) In September 1961, Jamaica held a _____ in which the people of Jamaica elected to pull out of the West Indian Federation.

e) By the 1970s, the Caribbean region was beginning to experience an increase in national consciousness, _____ and pride.

f) In 1962, Dr Eric Williams became the first Prime Minister of

_____.

g) In 1966 Errol W. Barrow became the first prime minister of

_____.

h) Grenada gained independence on 7th February _____.

i) Dominica gained independence in November _____.

k) In _____ St Lucia and St Vincent gained independence.

9 Is voting an important responsibility for a citizen? Do you think it should be legally required? Write 250 words expressing your ideas.

Think about:

- the struggle people had to gain adult suffrage

- how long it took for people to get the vote

- how it showed progress on the path to self-government for Caribbean countries.

Add any other ideas of your own.

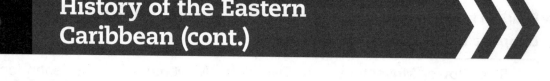

10 Read the key vocabulary in Unit 9 in the Student's Book. Then find the words in the word search puzzle below. The words can be horizontal, vertical or diagonal and backwards or forwards. There are 14 words to find.

K	S	R	J	W	H	F	E	I	H	S	H	X	L	G	Q	N	D	C	S	O	L	D	M
Y	U	Y	G	P	E	Z	F	F	U	B	Y	O	R	H	X	E	V	L	B	C	T	O	M
M	D	X	N	C	A	H	S	O	N	B	B	L	A	C	K	P	O	W	E	R	N	Y	P
N	G	C	F	Z	H	T	N	U	T	O	L	D	S	T	E	U	A	X	E	U	K	X	H
H	Q	M	Y	M	X	E	R	P	C	Q	Q	O	Z	D	C	L	J	M	M	T	J	Z	R
O	I	N	D	Q	G	K	O	I	K	Y	C	J	E	E	N	G	L	E	V	J	J	O	M
W	A	X	A	I	B	C	H	V	O	I	Y	Z	H	M	E	D	N	L	J	Y	Z	S	K
H	P	T	D	Z	M	Y	O	Q	A	T	Z	A	U	O	D	T	B	W	J	Y	E	Y	B
E	T	N	H	U	C	V	R	L	O	H	I	U	L	C	N	O	N	S	D	M	P	E	T
H	I	I	V	O	L	M	J	J	H	T	R	S	J	R	E	Q	R	F	G	W	R	P	T
S	L	L	U	F	F	U	I	R	Z	M	D	P	M	A	P	F	U	R	I	O	O	R	M
H	N	I	A	Q	S	A	X	J	R	M	N	G	U	C	E	G	Q	H	J	T	T	M	Y
A	G	B	E	T	S	E	L	M	Q	H	Q	O	Q	Y	D	W	C	H	Y	L	E	X	D
Q	V	L	I	V	D	Z	O	L	C	O	L	J	I	K	N	S	U	Y	A	H	S	E	T
A	D	C	B	C	B	Y	K	B	E	Q	E	X	E	T	I	M	D	R	B	N	T	L	A
R	E	H	P	K	E	V	X	A	A	G	M	P	D	M	A	C	D	H	D	G	A	T	N
I	C	Y	T	I	N	U	L	A	N	O	I	G	E	R	A	P	Y	T	O	D	N	A	I
P	U	D	E	A	B	T	B	I	J	K	V	A	G	I	O	L	I	H	G	I	T	E	X
U	M	R	S	S	U	U	Q	L	A	U	Q	O	N	R	D	C	S	C	C	Q	I	D	V
K	G	J	L	O	G	D	X	E	Q	Q	Y	R	J	C	V	N	U	I	N	S	S	I	Y
Q	D	C	A	G	G	C	D	R	V	A	O	Z	D	K	E	S	Y	R	A	A	M	R	J
M	S	I	U	D	N	I	H	S	F	X	L	M	Y	V	T	T	X	W	Z	D	M	P	U
K	D	L	T	F	C	W	S	S	L	O	W	W	L	J	F	W	O	V	Q	K	W	E	N

11 Now write the words in alphabetical order.

a) _____   b) _____

c) _____   d) _____

e) _____   f) _____

g) _____   h) _____

i) _____   j) _____

k) _____   l) _____

m) _____   n) _____